W9-BBN-037

A Look at Japan

by Helen Frost

Consulting Editor: Gail Saunders-Smith, Ph.D.

Consultant: Mark Ravina, Associate Professor,
specializing in Japanese History
Department of History, Emory University
Atlanta, Georgia

Pebble Books

an imprint of Capstone Press
Mankato, Minnesota

Pebble Books are published by Capstone Press
151 Good Counsel Drive, P.O. Box 669, Mankato, Minnesota 56002
http://www.capstone-press.com

1 2 3 4 5 6 07 06 05 04 03 02

Library of Congress Cataloging-in-Publication Data
Frost, Helen, 1949–
    A look at Japan / by Helen Frost.
    p. cm.—(Our world)
    Includes bibliographical references (p. 23) and index.
    Summary: Simple text and photographs depict the land, animals, and people
of Japan.
    ISBN 0-7368-1168-0
    1. Japan—Pictorial works—Juvenile literature. [1. Japan.] I. Title. II. Our world
(Pebble Books)
DS806 .F76   2002
952—dc21
                                                                    2001003308

The author thanks the children's section staff at the Allen County Public Library in
Fort Wayne, Indiana, for research assistance.

Note to Parents and Teachers

The Our World series supports national social studies standards
related to culture. This book describes and illustrates the land,
animals, and people of Japan. The photographs support early
readers in understanding the text. The repetition of words and
phrases helps early readers learn new words. This book also
introduces early readers to subject-specific vocabulary words, which
are defined in the Words to Know section. Early readers may need
assistance to read some words and to use the Table of Contents,
Words to Know, Read More, Internet Sites, and Index/Word List
sections of the book.

Table of Contents

Japan

★Tokyo

Japan is a country in eastern Asia. Japan has four main islands and many small islands. The capital of Japan is Tokyo.

Japan's flag

coast

plains

forest

6

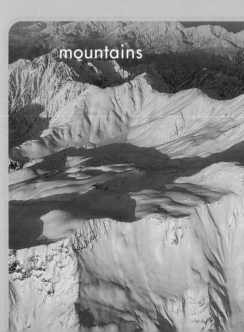

mountains

Japan has coasts, plains, forests, and mountains.
Japan is colder in the north than it is in the south.

snow monkeys

sea lion

Snow monkeys, deer, and wild boars live in Japan's forests. Sea lions and turtles swim near Japan's coasts.

More than 126 million people live in Japan. Most people live in cities near the coasts. People in Japan speak Japanese. They use symbols to write this language.

hello	good-bye
今日は	さようなら
koh-NEE-chee-wah	sah-yoh-NAR-a

Rice, noodles, and fish are the main foods of Japan. Japanese people use chopsticks to eat.

Japanese people celebrate
Children's Day on May 5.
They hope for the health
and happiness of all
children on this day.

Japanese factory workers make cars, cameras, and video games to earn money. Farming and fishing also are important jobs in Japan.

Japan's money is counted in yen.

Japanese people travel by bike, car, bus, and train. Some trains travel so fast that they are called bullet trains.

Mount Fuji is the tallest mountain in Japan. Mount Fuji is a volcano. The last time it erupted was 1707.

chopsticks—two narrow sticks used to eat food; chopsticks are used mostly by people in Asian countries.

coast—land next to the sea

island—land surrounded by water; Japan has four main islands and many small islands.

language—the words and grammar that people use to talk and write to each other; the Japanese language is made up of symbols that stand for words and phrases.

plain—a large, flat area of land

snow monkey—a monkey that lives in Japan's mountains; snow monkeys have red faces; they also are called macaques.

Tokyo—the capital city of Japan; Tokyo is the largest city in Japan; more than 34 million people live in Tokyo.

volcano—a mountain with vents; Mount Fuji is a volcano in Japan; Mount Fuji is 12,387 feet (3,776 meters) above sea level.

Read More

Britton, Tamara L. *Japan.* The Countries. Edina, Minn.: Abdo Publishing, 2000.

Kalman, Bobbie. *Japan: The Culture.* Lands, Peoples, and Cultures Series. New York: Crabtree Publishing, 2001.

Sinnott, Susan. *Japan.* First Reports. Minneapolis: Compass Point Books, 2001.

Witherick, M. E. *Japan.* Country Studies. Chicago, Heinemann Library, 2000.

Internet Sites

Japan
http://www.infoplease.com/ipa/A0107666.html

Kids Web Japan
http://jin.jcic.or.jp/kidsweb

Kids Window—Japan
http://www.jwindow.net/KIDS

Zoom School: Japan
http://www.enchantedlearning.com/school/Japan/index.html

Index/Word List

Word Count: 185
Early-Intervention Level: 17

Editorial Credits

Mari C. Schuh, editor; Kia Bielke, cover designer; Jennifer Schonborn, production designer and illustrator; Kimberly Danger and Alta Schaffer, photo researchers

Photo Credits

Betty Crowell, 14
Digital Stock, 1
Fritz Pölking/Visuals Unlimited, 8 (left)
International Stock/Miwako Ikeda, cover
Peter Essick/Aurora, 6 (lower right)
PhotoDisc, Inc., 8 (right), 20
Photo Network/Chad Ehlers, 6 (upper left), 10, 16
Prance/Visuals Unlimited, 6 (lower left)
Trip/N. Kealey, 6 (upper right); C. Rennie, 12; M. Fairman, 18